MY GURUJEE
PT. PHIROZ DASTUR

Pt. Sujan Rane

Author's Tranquility Press
MARIETTA, GEORGIA

Pt. Sujan Rane/Author's Tranquility Press

239 Richmond Dr Hiram,
GA 30141, USA
www.authorstranquilitypress.com

Ordering Information:
Quantity sales. Special discounts are available on quantity purchases by corporations, associations, and others. For details, contact the "Special Sales Department" at the address above.

Press On: Determination that Defies
My Gurujee Pt. Phiroz Dastur/Pt. Sujan Rane.

Paperback 978-1-959579-94-6
EPUB 978-1-959579-95-3

DEDICATION

I am proud to dedicate this book to the memory of my Gurujee Pt. Phiroz Dastur

ACKNOWLEDGEMENT

I am grateful to the following eminent persons in the field of Hindustani Classical Music, for their wholehearted contributions to this book, in the form of their articles.

Pt. Arvind Parikh, well-known Sitarist and
a desciple of Ustad Villayat Khan, Bombay, India.
Dr. Suresh Chandvankar, Hon. Secretary,
Society of Indian Record Collectors, Bombay, India.
Ustad Mashkoor Ali Khan, Faculty Member,
ITC Sangeet Research Academy, Calcutta, India
Pt. Ramdas Bhatkal of Popular Prakashan Pvt. Ltd. Bombay, India.
Dr. Keshavchaitanya Kunte, Head of Music Department,
Poona University, Poona, India.

FOREWORD

I have written this book with the intention of expressing my devotion to my Gurujee Pt. Phiroz Dastur. A doyen of the Kirana Gharana and a Torch-bearer, particularly of the Ustad Abdul Karim Khan Style of singing. One who commanded popularity, as a singer, right from his young age in 1931 to the present times. It is not common to come across a teacher of his calibre, particularly with the honesty and love he taught his every student for years. I happened to be one of them. I consider myself fortunate to be blessed to have had a teacher like him right from 1965 to 1995, though with some intermittent gaps due to my trips outside India and his too, because of his trips to USA during every summer. To accompany him on the Stage while he was singing was indeed a matter of great experience.

I also wish to thank my wife Neelima who has been a source of encouragement and support at every stage of this book.

In conclusion, may I share my experience with the readers, particularly the music-loving ones and students of the Hindustani Classical Vocal Music genre.

Pt. Sujan Rane
149 Cranbury Neck Road
Cranbury
New Jersey - 08512
USA
Email: panditsujanrane@gmail.com

Table of Contents

DEDICATION I

ACKNOWLEDGEMENT III

FOREWORD V

C H A P T E R   O N E 1

C H A P T E R   T W O 17

C H A P T E R   T H R E E 25

C H A P T E R   F O U R 27

C H A P T E R   F I V E 43

C H A P T E R   S I X 49

CHAPTER ONE

It was around 1955, I was sitting on a bench in front of a restaurant in a religious place called Shirdi in Maharashtra, India, and I heard a voice singing in utter pathos on the All India Radio Station of Bombay the favourite, Raag Abhogee Kanada of the Kirana Gharana. There are four major styles of singing in the Hindustani Classical Vocal Music, namely Gwalher, Agra, Jaipur and Kirana. The singers of these Gharanas had settled in those cities, after which these Gharanas assumed their names. Each of these Gharanas has contributed substantially to the development of Khayal Gayakee in the Classical Vocal Music genre. Here, something needs to be said in brief about Kirana Gharana, its lineage and its contribution to the Hindustani Classical Music. Kirana Gharana was popularized by Ustad Abdul Karim Khan in the last century. He was a Court Singer of the Maharaja of Gaikwad of the erstwhile State of Baroda. One of his duties was to teach Tarabai the daughter of Sardar Mane, brother-in-law of the Maharaja. In course of time a love affair developed between the Khansaheb and the daughter. But it was difficult for the love affair to come to fruition in the then conservative society of India, particularly bewteen a Muslim Singer and his Hindu disciple. Therefore, they eloped to Bombay and got married there. Soon they were blessed with gifted children, Sureshbabu Mane, his brother (name not known) Kamlabai, Hirabai and Saraswatibai. They came into limelight as successful singers in their own right. Especially Hirabai Badodekar, as she was then known, became a much successful singer and became one of the Torch-bearers of Kirana Gharana. This Gharana produced great singers like Sawai Gandharva (Rambhau Kundgholkar), Pt. Balkrishnabuwa Kapileshwari, Pt. Sangameshwar Gurav, Pt. Vishwanathbuwa Jadhav, Pt. Beherebuwa, Pt. Muley. Bharat-Ratna Pt.Bhimsen Joshi, Smt. Gangubai Hangal, Pt. Phiroz Dastur, Pt. Basawraj Rajguru etc. In short this Gharana has produced a linage of illustrious singers. The Gharana is known for being tuneful as its principal characteristic, for which the practitioners devoted years to develop correct musical Notes in their presentation. No wonder this Gharana has been favourite with the lovers of Hindustani Classical Vocal Music.

As said above, I was with my uncle in that religious place, called Shirdi, during my school days then. The singer was pouring out his feelings, in grief, so to say. The voice sounded similar to that of the immortal Ustad Abdul Karim Khan of the Kirana Gharana. I was eagerly waiting for the announcement at the end of the recital. It was announced that Pt. Phiroz Dastur of the same Gharana was presenting Raag Abhogee Kanada. I was simply amazed to listen, that a Parsee singer could sing that Raag with such a finesse and uncommon intensity. Generally, in this genre either Hindu or Muslim singers have made their mark, but a Parsee singer to carve a niche for himself was not known. Parsees, though a small community, have contributed significantly, not only in the commercial world of India, but also in the cultural one, especially in the world of Drama, Films and Music. Right from 1850 to 1930 many Parsee Dramatic Companies were in existence. In the earlier days they were owned by one Gustadjee Dalal, Dadabhai Naorojee and so on. Plays like "Deel Farosh" and "Gulnaar Firoz" were put on the stage. In this context, it would be appropriate to mention Imperial Movietone owner Mr. Ardesheer Irani, Wadia Movietone owner J.B. H. Wadia and his brother Homi Wadia, Minerva Movietone Sohrab Modi and Madan Theater's J.J. Madan, Mr. Ardesheer Irani was the producer of the first Talkie Film "Alam Ara" in 1931, in fact he introduced a new chapter in the history of the Indian Cinema by switching over from the era of Silent Films to Talkie Films. The first song recorded in that Film was "De De Khuda Ke Naam Par" sung by Wazeer Mohamed. Soon Talkie Films became the principal form of entertainment. Sulochana (an Anglo-Indian, Ruby Meyers), D. Billimoriya, Master Vithhal, and Zubeda (Wife of Maharaja Dhanrajgirjee of Hyderabad) came into limelight. In course of time they were followed by the blind singer K.C. De (Playback singer Manna De's uncle) Kundanlal Saigal, Ashok Kumar and Devika Rani. Film Music of those days, was largely based on Hindustani Classical Music.

My uncle Suryakant Rane was the first Music Director of the Indian Cinema (Ref. "75 Glorious Years of Indian Cinema" by Rajendra Oza of erstwhile Screen Publications of Bombay) who had set music for the Film "Veer Abhimanyu" in 1931 and followed it by another 20 Films in course of time. (Ref.–Film Music Research Scholar Mr. Harmandir Hamraz of Canpur, U.P., India). Some of the Parsees who contributed substantially to the Hindustani Classical Music in the last century, have been Pt. Jal Balaporia of Gwalher Gharana, Sarod Player Smt. Zarin Daruwaala and Tabla Maestro Smt. Aban Mistri Prabhat Pictures in Poona, Jayprabha and Prafulla Pictures in Kolhapur, New Theaters and Madan Theaters in Calcutta, Pancholi Arts in Lahore and Ranjeet Movietone and Bombay Talkies in Bombay soon followed Ardesheer Irani or around that time. Pt. Dastur's father Bejanji Dastur was fond of Hindustani Classical Music and regularly held recitals at his place in Bombay. During one of the recitals, the owner of Wadia Movietone, J.B. H. Wadia came in contact with Pt. Phiroz Dastur and was so impressed by the quality of his voice that he introduced young Dastur in a principal role in the Film World in his Film "Lal- Ye-Yaman" Mr. Wadia did not stop there but had all the other songs in that Film recorded in the voice of Dastur. His songs "Khalik Tori Najariya" and "Jawo Sidharo Fateh Pawo" became a hit. In 1938 Pt Dastur's father

Bejanji produced a Film called "Sunhere Baal". In this Film Pt. Dastur had set music. In 1940 he acted in another Film titled "Pak Daman" and in 1942 in "Return of Toofan Mail" where the music was set by Gyan Dutt and the song "Mat Ro Mat Ro Mard Kahanewale" became quite popular. In 1945 Pt. Dastur got an opportunity to act in the Film "Sharbati Ankhe". Music was arranged by Firoz Nizami of Lahore and the songs "Bikhare Kitane Roop Jagat Me" and "Ram Bade Gazab Ki Naar" once again was a talk of the town. One important fact needs to be mentioned here, is that Pt. Dastur sang in a duet with Lata Mageshkar, in a Film called "Bhairavi" produced by Dinkar Patil. Somehow, Lata was not comfortable to sing with Dastur and her song had to be separately recorded later. There is no documentary proof of this event but my Gurujee Pt Dastur himself told me this story, during one my teaching sessions.

The recital I had heard of Pt. Dastur, on the All India Radio Station of Bombay, in Shirdi left me quite restless for days, simply because I wanted to learn from him, though I had started my Taalim (Training) from a Gwalher Gharana singer known as Pt. Govind Prabhu, a Shagird (Disciple) of well-known singer Pt. Miraashibuwa. My training was followed through another singer called Pt. Rajarambuwa Jadhav of Kirana Gharana, whose father Pt. Vishwanathbuwa Jadhav of Kolhapur was a direct Shagird of Abdul Karim Khan, along with famed Sawai Gandharva, (Rambhau Kundgholkar), Pt. Mulebuwa, Pt. Beherebuwa and Pt. K.D. Jawkar.

Ustad Abdul Karim Khan
(1872 - 1937)

Smt. Hirabai Badodekar of Kirana Gharana
(1905 - 1989)

Pt. Bhimsen Joshi of Kirana Gharana
(1922 - 2011)

My thirst for the Kirana Gaykee, especially, of the Abdul Karim Khan type continued for a number of days, until I came across information about a Mehphil at Laxmi Baug, near Bombay's Opera House Theater, where Pt. Phiroz Dastur was to sing. The concert was in honour of a Tabaljee and some singers sang as a sign of respect for him. At the end of the concert, at about five in the early morning, Pt. Phiroz Dastur came on the stage, with an unusual calmness on his face. With no facial or physical movements he began Raag Komal Rishabh Asavari, the very Mukhda (Beginning of the Composition) was so captivating that it was sort of engraved on my mind and it has continued to be so for almost 50 years. The composition was "Preet Na Kije Kahu Sang Balama" which was taught to him by his Guru Sawai Gandharva. I showed no patience in learning it from Pt. Dastur in course of time.

Pt Sujan Rane (Writer of this book)

CHAPTER TWO

Pt. Phiroz Dastur was a child prodigy. He was born in a Parsee family in Bombay on 30th September 1919. He came into limelight as a child actor in Wadia Movietone Films in 1930's. Under J.B.H. Wadia he acted in his first Film Lal-Ye-Yaman. In the following years he acted in the undermentioned Films,

Lal-Ye-Yaman	1933
Bag-E-Misar	1934
Kala Gulab	1934
Dharmaki Devi	1935
Noor Yaman	1935
Prem Ratri	1936
Sher Ka Panja	1936
Sunhera Bal	1938
Sharbati Ankhe	1945

…but his soul lay in Hindustani Classical Vocal Music, especially in the Abdul Karim Khan type of Music. Probably his high-pitched voice was more suitable for this kind of Music and in no time he was drawn towards it. The notable fact in this regard was his Taalim, he had received it from the three eminent disciples of Abdul Karim Khan, Sawai Gandharv, Balkrishnabuwa Kapileshwari and K.D. Jawkar. It is recorded that Sawai Gandharva came to his house and taught him there, which was unlike the Taalim of the two well-known disciples Smt. Gangubai Hangal and Pt. Bhimsen Joshi who had to travel quite a distance to learn from him. In fact Sawai Gandharva made Pt. Bhimsen Joshi wait for a year or so until he was sure that the latter was bent on learning his Gayakee. It is interesting to note that when he travelled by a Train for his first public performance at Karachi in 1940, he had with him none other than the well-known singers Ustad Faiyyaz Khan, Smt. Gangubai Hangal and Pt. Kumar Gandhrava. The organizer at the Karachi concert unintentionally omitted to announce his name, but Ustad Faiyyaz Khan was quick enough in reprimanding them. He said to them in Hindi "Kyu Bhai Pt. Dasturka naam kyu nahi liyaa gayaa, kyu kee wo jawan hay?" (Why Pt. Dastur's name was not announced, was it because he is young?). The organizers readily admitted their error and quickly announced Pt. Dastur's name soon after. Pt Dastur himself narrated this story to me personally in one of my training sessions. This proves that even at that early age he was held in great esteem by other well-established singers of the time.

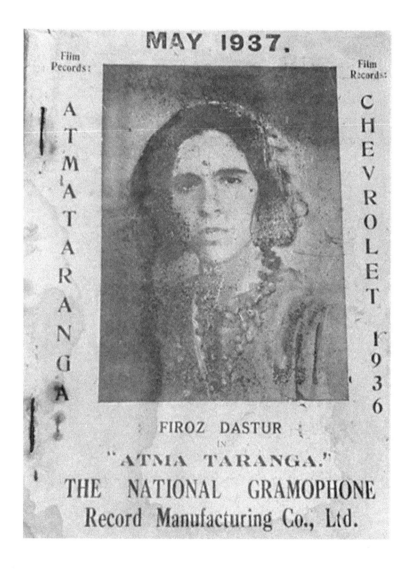

Pt. Dastur's photo on a Film Pamphlet

My urge to learn from Pt. Dastur never ebbed, but how and where to find him was the problem. I did not know anything about him. I had only seen him at Laxmi Baug concert and his fair-looking image was in my mind. One day as I was in the commercial area of Fort of Bombay, I happened to spot him. I walked towards him briskly and introduced myself with whatever modesty I could summon. He said he was a professional singer and hardly taught anybody, however he called me to his residence at Dubash Building in the Grant Road area of Bombay on one Sunday morning. I went to his apartment at the decided time. He asked me to sing something in order to ascertain if it would be worthwhile to take up my tuition. With great trepidation I sang the popular composition "Bhavanda Yaarada Jobana" in Raag Lalat, telling him at the same time that I was totally unaware of the Notes in it. To my luck and great happiness, he agreed to teach me. He started with the composition "Ab More Ram Biram" in Raag Gujri Todi. I had not heard of this composition before, but I was familiar with Abdul Karim Khan's "Begun Gun Gaye Allah Ke Saamane Jab Jayenge Tab Puchenge Ye Baat" and somehow to his understanding, managed it fairly well, simply because I was familiar with the Notes in the Gujri Todi of Abdul Karim Khan's well-known record. My Taalim began and continued till about 1995 or so. Of course there were intermittent gaps because of my trips outside India, besides he never used to teach during summer, as he was used to going to USA to stay with his nephew Rusi Dastur in Philadelphia. My Taalim went on in that manner but I remember with what love and dedication he taught me, never losing his cool inspite of my several faults and foreign assignments. He continued to teach me Raag "Yaman" for a year, drawing my attention and pointing out how I should proceed from one Note to another, touching a Note and staying on it after that, until I reached the upper Saa (Shadaj). This was the famous Kirana Gharana Badhat (Progression) which Abdul karim Khan's son Sureshbabu Mane, Hirabai Badodekar,

Saraswati Bai Rane and many other singers in that Gharana followed with ease and noticeable composure in their presentation.

CHAPTER THREE

My contemporaries or disciples who were trained by my Gurujee at that time, were Wagle, Sudha Divekar, Achyut Abhyankar and Raja Upadhye. If I remember correctly all of us were trained at Gurujee's apartment at Dubash Building, near Grant Road area of Bombay, while others were trained by him, in course of time, at the Bombay University's Music Department near Churchgate Railway Station. They did fairly well in their own way while presenting the Bandishes (compositions) taught by him. Another competent disciple here was Usha Deshpande who replaced him at his University assignment during his stay in USA. Sometime then, while he was engaged by the University to coach students there, I was tempted to ask him if I could join a Course there to learn singing. Without hesitation, he said "Rane do you want a piece of paper (Diploma in Music) or to learn how to become a singer." He was so truthful, even at the cost of his engagement there. This was sheer honesty for which he was too well-known everywhere in the music world of Bombay. He was on the Teaching Faculty of the Music Department of Bombay University right from its inception in 1969 till 2003. He was requested by the well-known Music Critic of the day Mr. Wamanrao Deshpande to accept a position in the Music Department of the University. The Head of the Music Department was Dr. Ashok Ranade a scholar of Hindustani Classical Music. Pt. Dastur taught at the Music Department for 34 years without a break. During this time he trained a number of students, who were lucky to receive Taalim from such an eminent Singer of Kirana Gharana. Taalim at his place was one of equally great experience and pleasure. He often made me wait after my tuition and with unusual pleasure invited me to join him for a dinner. Of course this was preceded by a peg or two of Whiskey, which I thoroughly enjoyed without any reservation. There was a wine shop below his apartment and he made a disciplined use of it. I understand many singers like the famous Ustad Rashid Khan frequented his place and enjoyed his company. On one occasion my Gurujee, Rashid Khan and I had a dinner at a restaurant in Girgaum, Bombay. I must say with pride, how lucky I was to have a dinner in the company of two stalwarts of the Classical Music. Once representatives of Doordarshn Bombay (Television) Station called at his place and offered to record his teaching session. Luckily, I was the student whom Datsur had selected and the Raag to be recorded was "Maru Behag" with the age-old composition "Rasia Ho Na Jaa" in Vilambit. At the appointed time the whole team of Doordarshan came to his apartment with their paraphernalia like Cameras, Flood Lights, and their Assistants. Pt. Dastur very calmly unfolded Raag Maru Behag, with the slightest idea on his face that his teaching was being recorded. He proceeded from one Note to another in a very professional manner, drawing my attention from time to time, to the slow progression of the Notes in that Raag. The Veelambit (Slow) composition of "Rasia Ho Na Ja" was followed by his own composition "Ras Bhare Tore Nainava, Manahari Lino Moraa" in the Drut Laya (Faster Tempo). We were informed later that the recording had been preserved in the New Delhi Archives of the All India Radio.

CHAPTER FOUR

In course of time, I started accompanying him at his recitals on the stage. Some of them I remember were at Bombay's St. Xavier's College, private recitals at Poona and even at the famed Abdul Karim Khan's Annual Memorial concerts at Meeraj in Maharashtra. I distinctly remember having sung Raag "Kedar" at Meeraj before him, which was followed by his presentation of Raag "Darbaaree" with unusual verve and pathos. It was an uncommon pleasure to listen to his "Darbaaree." This was during the period 1998-2002. One of the Mehfils where I had accompanied him was at a Maharaja's residence at Bombay's prestigious Malbaar Hill area. If I remember right he had presented a composition in Raag "Patdeep," being Dhan Dhan Ghariye..." and Abdul Karim Kham's popular Thumri "Jadu Bhareli Kaun Alabeli Ki Naina Rasile." There were hardly any audience there. Perhaps the Maharaja did not want anyone around him at the recital which he wanted to enjoy solely for his pleasure. It was a great experience. Then followed a concert at the well-known Sawai Gandgarva Annual Music Festival at Poona, in 1998, where I must say I was lucky enough to a company him. Pt. Bhimsen Joshi was unwell and therefore Pt. Dastur was the last singer to sing on the stage. He presented Raag "Bilaskhani Todi" with such a feeling that it was impossible to describe it. Here one noteworthy event deserves to be mentioned and that was his unfogettable presentation of Abdul Karim Khan's immortal Thumari "Gopala Meri Karuna Kyu Nahi Awe" which the music lovers of Poona rather compelled him to sing, even till his last recital, a few years before his death in 2008.

Pt. Phiroz Dastur with Pt. Sujan Rane at
latter's residence in Bombay, India in 1965

Pt Sujan Rane with Pt. Phiroz Dastur at his
residence in Bombay, India 2006.

Pt Sujan Rane singing at Tata Institute
of Fundamental Research, Bombay, India in 2010

Pt. Sujan Rane singing at the Annual Abdul
Karim Khan Music Festival at Meeraj, India in 1999

Pt Phiroz Dastur with Pt. Sujan Rane and
Pt Shrikant Deshpande (Sawai Gandharva's grandson),
in the Green Room before Sawai Gandharva's Music Festival
in Poona—1998

Pt Sujan Rane accompanying Pt. Phiroz Dastur at
Sawai Gandharva Music Festival, Poona, India in 1998

Pt Sujan Rane singing at Benares Hindu University,
Varanasi, India, Annual Concert in 2014

CHAPTER FIVE

In the midst of my strong desire to learn Hindustani Classical Vocal Music, I was also drawn towards Marathi Stage Music. I never lost an opportunity to listen to such stalwarts as Shripad Nevrekar of Goa and his nephew Ramdas Kamat. Suresh Haldankar was another Marathi Stage singer from Goa who appealed to me because of his very high-pitched and tuneful voice. But above all these singers, the actor—singer who impressed me most was Swararaj Chhota Gandharva. I was enamoured by his style of presenting Marathi Stage songs. He was named Chhota Gandharva after the celebrated Marathi Stage singing actor Bal Gandharva who had dominated the Marathi Stage from early 1900 to 1945 , with his utterly sweet and emotional manner of singing. Chhota Gandharva ruled the Marathi Stage from 1945 to 1970. He had an extremely sweet voice which impressed listeners in no time. Chhota Gandharva had also received Taalim for a while, from Sawai Gandharva, the Guru of Pt. Phiroz Dastur, Pt. Bhimsen Joshi and Smt Gangubai Hangal. I had heard Chhotaa Gandharva's Marathi Musical Play "Manapman" fifteen times at Shivaji Mandir Theater of Dadar, Bombay. His Marathi Stage songs "Dehata Sharanangata", "Ya Nav Naval Nayanotsva" "Prem Bhave Jeev Jagiya Natala" etc. were the hallmarks of Marathi Stage Music. Here I wish to indulge in a slight deviation in the sense that Chhota Gandharva was to sing at Bal Mohan Vidya Mandir School of Shivaji Park, Dadar, and Bombay around 1965. The organizers were looking for someone who could accompany him on the stage, with a Tambora. I was in the initial stage of learning Hindustani Classical Vocal Music but someone spotted me and asked me to be on the stage behind Chhota Gandharva, to support him on the Tambora. I was full of diffidence, as it was not a joke to accompany him , besides he sang at "E," while I was used to singing at "D," (One Note higher than mine). I thought he might sing for an hour or two, but he went on singing for almost four hours and my fingers were aching, because of playing the Tambora continuously. I was impressed beyond words and requested him at the end of the concert, if I could visit him at his house in Poona. He readily agreed and I went on to see him in course of time. I had a discussion with him, mentioning my Taalim with Pt. Dastur but expressed my desire to learn Natyasangeet from him, especially in his unique style. He had respect for Pt. Dastur and recommended that I should continue with him, but said because of his age he had stopped teaching anyone at his house. However he welcomed me and asked me to visit him at Bharat Gayan Samaj, Poona. But the arrangement did not work out, as he was in Poona and I was residing in Bombay, besides the distance between the two cities came in my way. When I asked him for his postal address, he said "Chhota Gandharva, Poona would suffice", that was the measure of his self-confidence. He sang with supreme confidence in his singing, so much so that other competent singers like Suresh Haldankar and Ramdas Kamat were nervous to sing in his presence on the stage. I was a witness to this sorry situation at the erstwhile King George High, Dadar, Bombay where his play "Saubhadra" was staged. Pt. Dastur excelled in singing Marathi Stage songs too. "Ugich Ka Kanta" and "Chandrika Hee Janoo" were his favourite songs.

As a follow up, I staged the Marathi Musical Play "Saunshay Kallol" at Bombay's Dinanath Natya Mandir, where I had played the main role of Ashween Sheth. The interesting feature of this event was that Pt. Dastur was the Chief Guest and it was a challenge for me act and sing before him, particularly when he was sitting right in the front row. But I think I did fairly well, which impressed him.

Pt. Phiroz Dastur as Chief Guest at Marathi Musical Play
at Bombay's Dinanath Natya Mandir in 1987, where Pt. Sujan Rane
had played the main role of Ashween Sheth

CHAPTER SIX

(My endeavours as a student of Hindustani Classical Music)

I taught Hindustani Classical Vocal Music in USA for almost ten years. My main aim was to propagate Kirana Gayaki, as I had learnt it from Pt. Dastur, but it was sad that because of their priorities students in USA never continued beyond a year or so. They were, perhaps, rightly in search of their progress at College level or in pursuit of commercial prospects thereafter. While I was going through this unfortunate experience I met with a serious car-accident, which took place in New Jersey as I was returning home, after my concert at Arshbodha (a religious place headed by a white American Sadhu) in 2004. I was thrown on a roadside, with a serious fracture of my left leg and had to be in bed for six months. It was difficult for me to pass such a long period in bed. I decided to write a book on Music, which could be used as a guide for prospective students of Hindustani Classical Vocal Music. I took quite a while to complete that book, but it was a fulfilling experience in the sense that my wife Neelima and I were invited by Cambridge University in UK in May 2018 in recognition of my contribution to Indian Music and the University accepted it for its library. In course of time this book was also accepted by Oxford University Library and the Library of U.S. Congress in Washington, USA.

I am happy to state that my book on Music was later accepted by Princeton University, Library, USA, Bombay University Library, Poona University Library and I.T.C. Sangeet Research Academy Library of Calcutta. It was accepted by N.C.P.A. Library, Bombay too.

I did not stop my endeavors here and pursued Hindustani Classical Music in another area. As I am also a well-recognized Portrait–Painter in USA, Middle East and India, I donated my oil portraits, including that of Pt. Dastur, to some of the well-known institutions in India. Among them were the Music Departments of Maharaja Sayajiraw University of Baroda, Benares Hindu University, Varanasi, Bombay University and Poona University. Perhaps in the Collectors' market in USA or elsewhere, I might have earned much more monetarily, but the honour of donating my oil portraits to these institutions, was of great value to me.

SUJAN Rane's photo at Cambridge University Library, UK in recognition and acceptance of his book " Learning Hindustani Classical Vocal Music "

Among the Awards which Pt. Dastur received in India, the following deserve mention.

1) Tansen Award in Music of the Madhya Pradesh Government
2) South Gujrat University Honarary D.Litt. in Music
3) Maharashtra Government Award in Music.
4) Sangeet Natak Academy of New Delhi Award in Music.

Pt Phiroz Dastur as a Teacher—

Pt Dastur's way of teaching was unique in the sense that he always insisted that if one Raag was not learnt correctly, the student might not learn other Raags well enough, at least in the Kirana way of singing. Consequently he taught a Raag in the beginning at least a year. In my case he taught me Raag "Yaman" for almost a year, the composition was the traditional one, being "Kay Sakhi Kaiseki Kariye Bhariye Din, Aiso Lalan Ke Sang—Asthai (First Half of the Composition)

"Sunahri Sakhi May Kaa Kahoo Tose Jaanat Unhike Dhang"— Antara (Second Half of the Composition)

I was soon bored, repeating the same words and the Aalaps of the Asthai and Antara over and over again. He reprimanded me by saying that I expected to know a Raag in six weeks, whereas Sawai Gandgarva taught him a particular Raag for at least six months. Repetition of Aalaps made them stronger in the student's mind and the student could always present them with confidence while singing on the stage. There was considerable sense and truth in his way of teaching, as I realised it in course of time. He was also very particular about the words in a composition, as they heightened the value of Aalaps and made them more appealing to the listeners. Similarly he was meticulous about Taans, which were few in his compositions, but were quite effective. He made students repeat them with the Notes, so that they could sing them flawlessly and with ease, in their performances. He was also particular about the Tabla Beats in a composition and held a Tabla (Dagga) in his hand and played the Beats so that the Students could learn the correct placement of words on the Beats. Besides, Pt. Dastur was careful about protecting the vocal chords of the student. He would hold a mirror in front of the student's open mouth and would show him the position of the tongue, often asking the student to keep his tongue flat touching the lower part of the mouth. This would help the student to open his mouth and sing in a full-throated voice. Pt. Dastur had attended some sessions in Voice Culture at Pt. B. R. Deodhar's Music classes at Opera House, Bombay.

Pt. Phiroz Dastur as a Singer–

Pt. Dastur was thinly built like Ustad Karim Khan as if to suit his body structure, he had a high-pitched tenor voice, which was well suited to his way of singing. Singers in his Gharana, like Sureshbabu Mane, Sawai Gandharva, Sangameshwar Guraw, Basawraj Rajguru and Pt. Yashwantrai Purohit had all high-pitched voices, which helped them considerably to present this Gayaki in all its faithfulness.

Pt. Dastur excelled in his performances and there were reasons for his success. He never bungled in his presentation. He proceeded systematically from one Note to another, almost caressing the Notes very gently. He was slow and calm in his presentation. He was never in a hurry to exploit Notes and cared for their true value, in a particular composition. Like his contemporaries, he never indulged in fast Taans, which were anathema to him. He was averse to showing off his artistry and was against facial contortions or physical jerks or histrionics to express his musical qualities. In fact he was seen as if beseeching Almighty's favours. Serenity was the hallmark of his singing. He distinguished between Notes with unusual correctness. For example the Dhaivat in Raag Todi or Dhaivat in Raag Darbaaree. Same reasoning went with Madhyam of Kalyan and Madhyam of Multani. He often presented Ustad Abdul Karim Khan's Thumaries with an unusual faithfulness. Though he imitated them gracefully and may have been criticized in doing so, there was a uniqueness in his presentation, inasmuch as he often added his own Aalaps and Taans. Khansaheb's Thumaries lasted hardly for four minutes in his famous records, while Pt. Dasturjee's presentation of each of them, lasted for fifteen minutes or so on the stage. His repertoire was not as extensive as that of his Gurubandhu Pt. Bhimen Joshi or his Gurubhagini Smt Gangubai Hangal, but whatever Raags or Thumaries he presented, kept the listeners glued to their seats in his every performance, simply because he was faithful to Khansaheb's Thumaries beyond imagination. Repetition of the Thumaries in every performance never mattered so much, as the manner in which he presented them with feeling and pathos. He was respected by his contemporaries so much that the popular singer like Ustad Rashid Khan came all the way from Calcutta and sang without any monetary compensation at Bombay's Dadar Matunga Cultural Center, singing Raag "Bridavani Sarang" in the afternoon and Raag "Patdeep" in the evening. Eminent singer like Pt. Bhuimsen Joshi and Music Director Shreenivas Khale were in the audience. He was equally humble in taking permission of important singers sitting before him for his recitals. In a concert where Ustad Niaz Ahmed, the last descendent of Kirana Gharana was present, he was quick enough in bowing to him and seeking his permission to sing. On another occasion when Jaipur Gharana's Smt Mogubai Kurdikar was in attendance at Dadar Matunga Cultural Center, he had the grace to seek her permission to begin his recital with Raag Lalat. This was a proof of his modesty.

On the eve of his 75th Birthday, he said in his interview at Bombay's Mahalaxmi Racecourse, " This Art needs purity of soul. ". It is not easy to understand the depth underlying this statement. He looked at his Music with a spiritual angle and only he could understand its intensity.

It is said that one needs to be fortunate to have a Guru like Pt. Dastur. It is abundantly so true in my case.

Pt. Dastur as a Human Being—

Pt. Dastur was too well known for his truly human qualities in the Music World of India. . He never spoke against the music performances of his fellow singers or criticized them. To prove this point I am tempted to quote my own experience. I was sent by him one evening to the former Municipal Commissioner Mr.Kale's House at Carmichael Road in Bombay, for a musical concert. The singer who was to sing at his place, was well-known but somehow his singing did not appeal to me and naturally I failed to appreciate the Raag " Miya Malhar " he had presented. On the following Saturday, when I was at Pt. Dastur's place for my Taalim, he asked me how did I find the singer's performance. I was honest enough in my opinion and said that at least the singer himself "understood" what he was singing. But Pt. Dastur had the big heart to say that unless I heard a singer for at least four times I should not form any opinion. He was so right in his judgement. Similarly, he was highly religious in his outlook. There was a small marble statue of the Saint Saibaba on a pedestal, just before the entrance to the Grant Road Market in Bombay, near his house. After leaving his apartment in the evening, he would invariably visit the Statue, remove his sandals, keep a coin or two in front of it, bow before it and pray. He was kind even to rodents and birds like crows near his apartment. He did not have the nerve to hurt them and often offered them food, though his habits appeared unhygienic to others.

He will undoubtedly go down in the history of Hindustani Classical Singers as one of the greatest singers of the Twentieth Century, who had made his mark in it right from his childhood.

Messages received from eminent persons in the field of Hindustani Classical Music.

Pt. Sujan Rane with Pt. Arvind Parikh

Message received from famous Sitarist
Pt. Arvind Parikh, disciple of Ustad Villayat Khan
May 10, 2022

At my age of 94, I find it difficult to assist you as desired. Phirozbhai was a wonderful musician of Kirana Gharana. My best wishes for a great success for your project."

Message received from
Dr. Suresh Chandvankar
Hon. Secretary, Society of Indian Record Collectors
Mumbai, India, May 23, 2022

Me and Music of Pt. Phiroz Dastur

Born and brought up in Sadashiv Peth of Pune, I lived very close to the venue of Sawai Gandharva festival that was held annually. However, I never attended it during my school and college days. But I used to go on the last day morning to join the crowd that would stand outside the gate to listen to Pandit Bhimsen Joshi's Marathi & Hindi Bhajans. In one such occasion around 1968, I went early morning and heard a thin high pitched female like voice of someone singing 'Gopala Karuna Kyun Nahi Aave'.

Asked the fellow listener standing next to me, I learned the name of the singer Pandit Firoz Dastur, disciple of Sawai Gandharva and that the song he was singing was ditto like Abdul Karim Khan Saheb. Honestly, I did not know any of these names that time. In 1975, I came to Mumbai for my first and last job at 'Tata Institute of Fundamental Research' with my small collection of gramophone records of film music. With frequent visit to Mumbai flea market called Chor Bazzar and meeting many collectors I began to collect and listen to the records of different genre and period. Child prodigy Master Firoz Dastur name appeared on early film music shellac discs labels. Upon inquiry with the senior collectors I came to know that he was he same person whom I had listened to in Pune festival. He learned the music of Kirana Gharana and emerged as a fine exponent under the guidance of Sawai Gandharva. Soon I collected many records of Kirana gharana singers and began to understand them with the help of seniors. Around 1990, record collectors in Mumbai formed a group, 'Society of Indian Record Collectors' and this led to much more interaction with the fellow record collectors in India and abroad. Very few shellac discs recordings of Master Firoz Dastur are surviving today. His music and concerts were also released on cassette tapes and compact discs during 1970—2000. In 1990, Mr. Siddhartha Kak produced a four part serial titled—Gaata Jaye Banjara' describing 1931 to 1990 period of Hindi Film music. Part one of this series had a long interview of Pandit Phiroz Dastur. He narrates about 1935–1940 period of his career as a child artist in early Talkie Films. I began to attend the seminars of music forum in Mumbai from 1990 onwards where I met Panditji for couple of times and talked with him about his early film recordings. But he was not much interested in them. Dawn of digital age made a real revolution. Now I can listen to all the available music of Pandit-ji anytime and anywhere I want. His long interviews and insightful information and analysis has added to my listening pleasure immensely. Like in the case of Ustad Abdul Karim Khan, I find both the male and female voice elements in the recordings of Pandit Phiroz Dastur. Among his big repertoire of recorded music, my most favourite raga is Gavati and I listen to it again and again.

Message received from
Ustad Mashkoor Ali Khan
Faculty Member, I.T.C. Sangeet Research Academy
Calcutta, India.
May 25, 2022.

PT . PHIROZ DASTUR BY USTAD MASHOOR ALI KHAN

Today I will say something about the singing style and nature of Pt Phiroz Dastur. Pt Phiroz Dastur was a senior and a good singer of Kirana Gharana. There was honesty in his Gayakee and hence it was glittering. It was simple and straightforward and Pt. Dastur saw a Raag in its right perspective. He was tuneful in his Akars, simple in his Taans and forceful in the throw of his voice. He never resorted to facial contortions and body movements to express his singing ability. His singing style was free from any faults connected with voice production. As I understand from my seniors he had received good Taalim (Training) from Sawai Gandharva. Listeners carried home the impression, at the end of his recitals that he belonged to the true Kirana Gayakee of the tradition of Abdul Karim Khan. This was the nature of his Gayakee. I remember that when I sang in Sajan Milap concert in 1984, Pt. Bhimsen Joshi, Gangubai Hangal, Niaz Ahmed and Faiyyaz Ahmed, Khadim Hussen Agrewale and Pt. Phiroz Dastur were present. My concert was successful and Pt Phiroz Dastur quickly walked up to the stage and complimented me. Pt Bhimsen Joshi sang after me. Pt. Dastur learned Raag Abhogee Kanada (Banara Rangila.....) and Puriya Dhanashri (Khwaja Qutubuddin Nawaz....) and some more Raags from Chhote Khan of Sarangpur. We often met at concerts at Hubli, Dharwad, Goa and Mumbai and exchanged compositions. Touching the heart of listeners was the true nature of his Gayakee.

Regarding his nature he was straightforward, simple and away from all kinds of Politics. Singing was his ultimate goal. He was pleasant and sweet in his conversations, there was no trace of any compulsion. In appearance he was fair and good-looking, with good features, always wearing white or light yellow dress. His Gayakee was free of any Tamasha (show) or facial changes or physical movements. In fact there are two types of singing styles which would leave listeners with the impressions of saying "Hi" or "Wah" at the end of concerts. Ustad Abdul Karim Khan, Ustad Wahid Khan, Sawai Gandharva, Beherebuwa, Roshanara Begum, Niaz Ahmed and Faiyyaz Ahmed, Manilk Verna, Prabha Atre and Pt. Phiroz Dastur sang "Hi" type of Gayakee which touched the soul of listeners. Such Singers are not born often. May the Almighty give peace to his soul, I am saying all this for my elder brother Pt Sujan Rane who loves me greatly. May God give him a long life. My blessings to him.

Message received from
Pt. Ramdas Bhatkal
Popular Prakashan Pvt. Ltd.
Bombay, India.
May 26, 2022.

PT. PHIROZ DASTUR BY RAMDAS BHATKAL

In my childhood I was exposed to Hindusthani Classical music. Those days it was not unusual for young kids to enjoy classical music, sometimes in concerts lasting till late into night or late afternoon without worrying too much about lunch or dinner.

Those days were dominated by the Gharana system, even after Vishnu Narayan Bhatkhande had consciously made attempts at erasing this distinction by printing compositions from different traditions in his six volumes of 'Kramik Pustak Malika.'

While I was close to music I was not close to musicians, especially those belonging to Gharanas other than Bhatkhande tradition. But thanks to my association, during my school days with Deodhar School of Music and Bharatiya Sangeet Shikshapeeth in Bombay I developed a catholic taste in Music I could appreciate recordings of great musicians irrespective of the traditions they belonged to.

At the Paluskar and Bhatkhande Anniversary programmes and at the concerts arranged by private clubs such as Suburban Music Circle I was able to listen to Pandit Phiroze Dastur. I had an ear for special qualities that were highlighted by different traditions. Pandit Dastur's keen sense of Sur (Note) had further piercing emotional impact as he sang from his heart. His command over the art and technique was obviously exemplary. Perhaps I was too uninstructed at that time to understand this aspect. But decades later his Jogia and Bhairavi still resonate in my ears. Later my own Taalim has been in different tradition, yet I try to sing 'Gopala' and 'Jamuna ke teer'and some of these compositions in his style.

I had the good fortune of knowing some of his distinguished disciples such as Milind Chittal, Vinayak Prabhu, Usha Deshpande and Sujan Rane who carry on this rich tradition.

Message received from
Dr. Keshavchaitanya Kunte
Head, Music Department,
University of Poona
Poona, India.
May 31, 2022.

Pandit Phiroz Dastur:
A creative musician within the tradition
Dr. K J Kunte

In Hindustani Art-music, especially in Khayal form, there has been always a tussle between tradition and experiment. Khayal music, being a more idiosyncratic mode of Raga presentation, is believed to have an innate quality of self-expression. This is why, most of the pioneers of Gharana-s of Khayal (i.e. stylistic idioms of Khayal singing) have explored the possibilities of experimentation and newness, and sometimes went on the level of a so-called rebel! But still, the continuity of tradition and maintaining the set of traditional aesthetic values is also an important task. One can largely classify the musicians into two categories—the traditionalists and experimenters. Pandit Phiroz Dastur was a major musician in the former category.

Being a traditionalist doesn't mean that the musician is not experimenting at all. Such experiments are within the norms of the tradition; they are on a micro-level. Pandit Dastur, one of the prominent Hindustani Khayal singers from the Parsee community in India, learnt under Pandit K D Jaokar, Pandit Sawai Gandharva and Pandit Balkrishna Kapileshwari. His musical icon was Ustad Abdul Karim Khan, the pioneer of Kirana Gharana. He not only worshipped Ustad's peculiar style of singing but also carried it forward and disseminated it to several students.

I can see three aspects of Pandit Dastur's musical personality— a performer, a composer and a Guru. Surprisingly, these are three different personalities within the same person! As a performer, he was a traditionalist. As a composer, he was aesthetically creative. And as a Guru, he was orthodox.

As a performer, he believed thoroughly in the aesthetic values of Kirana tradition. His voice was naturally sweet and lucid, with a little feminine softness. But he took efforts in making it capable of rendering Ustad's Gayaki (singing style). Though in the early decades of his life, he was a child prodigy actor-singer, later he focused only on Khayal music and never sang any forms other than Khayal, except Thumri and

Thumri style Bhajan. (How can one forget his emotionally immersed rendition of 'Gopala Meri Karuna Kyo Nahi Ave'?)

Keeping the thrust on Khayal singing, he demonstrated the 'Badhat Ang' in Khayal exploration (note-by-note progression in presenting Raga) which is a forte of Kirana tradition. The gradual, slow-paced elaboration of the Raga, highlighting the emotive quality, and nuanced expression of the Raga-mood with peculiar Shruti-Sthana (microtonal rendition) were some prominent features of Dastur Ji's Khayal vocalism. His Alap-s were soothing, meditative. His Bol-Ang was appealing. His Taan patterns were forceful, but not too aggressive or jarring. He was always successful in maintaining an overall introvert, pensive impression; with avoiding vigorous, robust or quixotic, over-alluring appeal. And this made his music more spiritual than entertaining. He was more a serious meditator than a gallery-playing entertainer.

He preferred Ragas such as Lalit, Bhairav, Todi, Shuddha Sarang, Multani, Patdeep, Marwa, Puriya Dhanashri, Yaman, Shuddha Kalyan, Darbari Kanada, Malkauns, Bahar, etc. which have a particular mark of Kirana tradition. He seldom explored complexly structured Ragas, Ragas with hurried movements, uncommon or Jod-Raga (mixture of Ragas). But it is interesting to note that he created a few new Ragas such as Kali-Bahar (combination of Ramkali and Bahar), Durga Malhar (which is a Jod-Raga), Chandramukhi (a type of Chandrakauns with the addition of Rishabh, the natural second tone, which is originally omitted in the Raga).

There was no highlighting emphasis on the rhythmic aspect in Dastur Ji's music as he preferred common Talas-Ektala, Teentala, Jhaptala and Rupaka, and he was not very keen on the syncopating patterns or rhythmic interplay. Though he was aware of the poetic content in the Khayal compositions, he used to rather focus on the Raga expression than the lyrical expression. So, the use of syllables in the Khayal poem was restricted to the enunciation of note-clusters and was not open to project poetic meaning. In this regard too, he followed the same strategy which Ustad Abdul Karim Khan favoured.

If one compares him with his two contemporary mates, i.e. Gangubai Hangal and Bhimsen Joshi, it is clear that he represented the style of Ustad Abdul Karim Khan and Sawai Gandharva with more original or faithful expression. The performing idiom of Gangubai Hangal and Bhimsen Joshi was more individualistic, but Dastur Ji kept Ustad's stylistic features intact and integral. This also might be a reason why he was a more successful as Guru, in comparison with two others. Dastur Ji passed on Kirana vocalism to a large scale by training almost two generations of singers—from Achyut Abhyankar, Sudha Divekar, Sujan Rane to Girish Sanzgiri, Shuchita Athalekar. His teaching methodology was very disciplined and elaborate, and he was a very patient teacher. One very rarely finds such a combination of a performer and an educator in a single person.

The Kirana tradition is blamed for not giving prominence to the 'Bandish' aspect and hence, we rarely find Bandishkar-s or Khayal composers in this tradition. But Dastur Ji being an exception was one of the early Khayal composers from this stream. He composed many Khayal compositions with a melodic intonation pertaining to the Kirana idiom. These compositions are simple on a general outlook but are rich in melodic content and they prove to be a good guideline for further Raga elaboration. That is why most of his compositions are largely in circulation for both- concert performances and teaching.

Pandit Phiroz Dastur was certainly a torchbearer of Kirana tradition in the 20th century, who was able to give a sublime musical experience with aesthetic fervour.

A few personal memories—

Pt. Dastur used to sing in 'Sawai Gandharva Sangeet Mahotsav', a celebrated music festival in Pune. As the festival is being held in memory of his Guru, his performance here had to have a special emotional touch. In this 3-night long festival, he would finish the second last night session. I fondly remember his renditions of many Ragas such Lalit, Todi, Ahir Bhairav, Bairagi, Jogiya. The audience used to enjoy his soulful rendition of 'Gopala Meri Karuna', and never let him get off the stage without singing this masterpiece. 'Soch Samajh Nadan' was his other favourite composition. Usually, before the performance, any singer practices in the greenroom and makes a point in submerging into the mood of the performance, with a little warmup. But I remember, many times Dastur Ji used to listen to other artists all night, go directly on the stage, and start singing without any frills. His performing character was simple, without pageantry or ostentation. But still, he would capture the hearts of the listeners with just a few notes. Such power of solemnity was in his musicAround 2007-2008, I was fortunate to visit his home a few times and have informal conversations with him. He was an 88-year old complete ripe Parsee gentleman and used to welcome youngsters like me with a bright cheerful grin. Though he was a thoroughly serious musician, as a person was convivial and jovial. His house was filled with musical vibrations–just like his tuneful Tanpuras! In the crowded, noisy Mumbai gully, his home was like a temple of pure music.

On one such visit, after musical discussions, we also had some natter. After spending some 2 hours, he offered me to have lunch with him. While having lunch, I asked him, "How come you have such positivity and freshness even at this age?" He smiled and asked, "It is all 'Guru-Krupa' (blessings of the master). And of course, the purity of music makes one pure by heart if you practice it with devotion and selflessness."

I owe my gratitude to my Gurujee, Pt. Phiroz Dastur, because by virtue of his Taalim (Training) I could present my recitals at the following places in the years to follow

LIST OF Pt.. SUJAN RANE'S CONCERTS

Indian Cultural Association, Muscat, Oman, 1978-83
Marathi Cultural Organization, London 1984.
Main roles in Marathi Musical plays Saunshay Kallol and
Manapaman in   Muscat,
Oman, 1982-83
Main role in Saunshay Kallol, Dinanath Natya Mandir, Bombay in
the presence of his
his Guruji Pt. Phiroz Dastur of Kirana Gharana, 1987.
Several Cultural associations in Bombay and Pune 1988-91.
Indian and Pakistani Cultural organizations in Al-Khobar, Saudi
Arabia 1992–1996.
Abdul Karim Khan Memorial concert at Meeraj, 1998.
Abdul Karim Khan Memorial concert at Meeraj 2001.
Arshabodh Ashram, Somerset, New Jersey, USA 2004
Dr. Geeta Ghanekar's residence, Edison, New Jersey, USA 2006.
Dr. Vijaya Murthi, Principal SIES College, Bombay, residence 2009.
Mr. Sadanand Yadvalkar CEO Reliance Petrochemicals, Bombay,
2009.
Rajhauns Trust, Goregaon,Bombay 2010.
Kala Academy, Goa 2010.
Tata Institute of Fundamental Research, Bombay 2010.
Kalashree Sangeet Mahotsav, Pune, 2011.
Swaragangotree, Goregaon, Bombay 2011.
Ram Mandir, Girgaum, Bombay 2011.
Mrs. Sushila Mehta, Agra Gharana Singer, Bangalore residence 2012.
Institute of World Culture, Bangalore 2012.
ITC Sangeet Research Academy, Calcutta 2012.
Kannan Sangeet Kunj, Calcutta 2013.

Shikshayatan Cultural Center, New York 2013.

Kirana Sangeet Academy, Bangalore 2013.

Benaras Hindu University, Varanasi Annual concert 2014.

Swanand Sangeet Mahotsav, Borivali, Bombay 2014.

Shiv-Vishnu Temple, Maryland, USA 2014.

Athashree Paranjpe Housing Complex, Pune 2014.

Anahatnaad Sangeet Mahotsav, Madgaon, Goa 2015.

Seniors 'Club, Borivali, Bombay 2015.

Upvan Sangeet Mahotsav, Thane sponsored by Times of India 2016.

Benaras Hindu University, Varanasi, centenary celebration 2016.

Vallabh Sangeeta lay, Sion, Mumbai December 2016.

Swar Sadhna Samiti, Mumbai February 2017

Amad Pratishtan, Santacruz, Mumbai, February 2017

Nehru Center, High Commission of India, London May 2018

Kusumohtsav Music Festival, Bridgewater Temple, New Jersey 2018

Benares Hindu University, Varanasi, India in March 2022.